Y

.HURCH COLLEGE

This item must be returned (or renewed) on or before
the last date indicated below.
Reserved items **must** be returned by the notified **recall**
date.

28. FEB 1997			an
1 5 OCT 2007			es

15103237

Church Information NZ

My name is Tony.
What's your name?
I'm here.
So are you!
I'm alive.
So are you!

I use my whole body
to communicate to
other people

I've got two eyes.
I can see with my eyes.
I can see my sister's doll.
I can see the tree outside our house.
What can you see?

I've got two ears.
I can hear with my ears.

I can hear Mum calling.
She is calling my little sister Ann.
I can hear our dog barking.
I can hear a car in the street.
What can you hear?

I've got a nose.
I can smell things with my nose.
I can smell the flowers on the table.
I can smell the dinner in the oven.
I can smell the soap that I wash with.
What can you smell?

I've got a mouth.
I can talk with my mouth.
I can eat with it too!
I can taste things.
An apple tastes sweet and crunchy.
I like the taste of baked beans.
What tastes do you like?

I've got two hands.
I can clap my hands.

I can build things with my hands.
I can draw and cut out pictures.
I can stroke our cat.
What can you do with your hands?

I've got two legs.
I can run with my legs.
I can jump and hop.
I can play football.
My sister Ann can skip.
What can you do with your legs?

We can do lots of nice things with our hands.
We can do nasty things, too.
We can punch somebody.
Or we can hug somebody.

Ann is hugging Judy,
because Judy fell down.

With our legs we can kick somebody.
Or we can walk home with our friends.
I am walking home with my friend Paul.

With our eyes we can look cross, like Ann.
But we can make our eyes smile, too.

Can you make your eyes
look cross?
Can you make your eyes smile?

With our mouths we can call people names.
But we can say nice things, too.

I am growing up.
I used to be very small.
I could not do very much.
Now I can do lots of things.
I can help other people.

Hands and legs and eyes are very useful.
We can use them all to make us happy.
We can use them all to help other people, too.

Here are Ann and Michelle.
They are using their hands
and legs and eyes to show
that they are friends.

Here I am!

Notes for parents and teachers:

The child's world is centred on himself. At first he learns to enjoy, and later to say 'Thank you' for, his own powers and abilities. Gradually he begins to understand that with growth comes greater responsibility and a need to consider and to care for others.

It is our task to introduce him—not through words or ideas which may be meaningless to him, but through simple, everyday experiences such as those shown in this book—to 'the quality of Christian living'; in other words, to introduce him to what life as a Christian is really about.

The book can be used as a basis for the child's own prayers of thanksgiving and intercession, and for talk together about our senses and abilities, how these give us pleasure and how they can be used.

Produced by arrangement with Nederlandsche Zondagsschool Vereeniging, Amsterdam
© English text: Central Board of Finance of the Church of England, 1975